D1038106

Presented

to

_____

_____

by

_____

_____

_____
DATE

GOOD MORNING, LORD

Five-Minute Devotions

Charles R. Hembree

BAKER BOOK HOUSE
Grand Rapids, Michigan

1 The Smallest Swindle

Suggested Scripture: Luke 16:1-13

Bilking consumers out of pennies has now become a billion-dollar business. The *National Observer* recently noted that short weighing on food, gasoline, home fuel oil, packaged hardware items, and pills cost the American public some six to twelve billion dollars per year. In an effort to curb this swindle, whether accidental or intentional, many states are spot-checking weights and measures.

Pennsylvania investigators discovered that 15.5 percent of all prepackaged foods checked were short weighted, with some stores shorting on 25 percent of the packages checked. A three-day Kansas investigation turned up evidence that 30 percent of all meat packaged in eleven stores were short weighted. In Arkansas, officials checked one-pound cans of vegetables to find none that contained sixteen ounces. And Tennessee officials found prepackaged pork chops short weighted by up to thirty-one cents. Officials have tabulated forty-eight ways to cheat in weighing meat in front of customers, and many markets are apparently using some of them.

All of this reveals the avarice deep within the hearts of men, as well as a basic dishonesty in our striving for materialistic gain. This cheating on small things seems to be tragic commentary on our society.

"Where does sin start?" seems to be a question

many are asking. Is it evil to cheat for pennies or does "right" have a price tag on it? Tragically, many feel the results of the smaller swindle area of our culture but hardly raise an eyebrow as it is perpetrated. Under-the-table deals and payoffs are often accepted in our society as we shrug our shoulders and let them go unnoticed.

Thoughtful people may ponder and debate where evil starts, but the Bible is very clear. Christ gave many parables about honesty and responsibility, declaring that man's avarice begins in the heart and does not have a price tag. It is just as dishonest to steal a penny as it is to steal a million dollars. Jesus said it this way: "He that is faithful in that which is least is faithful also in much: and he that is unjust in the least is unjust also in much" (Luke 16:10). Many of our nation's youth have become disenchanted with our moral values because they seem to be on a sliding scale. Situational ethics is really no ethics at all. Jesus drew the line between good and evil very clearly, and said boldly for us to get on one side or the other. Unlike earthly teachers, God does not grade on a curve.

Trying to excuse our small dishonesties, we often say, "At least I haven't murdered, committed adultery, or robbed a bank." Yet one does not have to break all the laws of the land to be considered a criminal. Similarly, one does not have to break every commandment to be a sinner. The Bible simply states, "For whosoever shall keep the whole law, and yet offend in one point, he is guilty of all" (James 2:10).

Four times in the Book of Proverbs it is noted,

"A false balance is abomination to the Lord: but a just weight is his delight." Obviously, honesty in the small things is important to our creator. Sin is a seed which grows until one day it overwhelms us. If we erase the mark between good and evil to inch it further with each situation, before long we find our own avarice has moved us to forget the line completely. Jesus clearly states that the time to stop evil is at its conception.

Stories of Abe Lincoln's honesty in walking miles to return a few pennies he overcharged warm our hearts, for we admire honesty. However, this should be the norm, with the dishonest being the exception. But when one steps out to be honest he is almost laughed out of the ball park.

If Christ cannot trust us with the little things, surely He cannot trust us with the bigger things. This means expense accounts, tax forms, and petty cash. Conversely, those who are honest and just in the little are those God trusts with the great things in His kingdom. If we are faithful in a few things, He will make us ruler over many.

2 "Because I Need You"

Suggested Scripture: John 3:1-17

A country doctor once told of a patient whose husband was a strong, taciturn man little given to expressing his feelings. The woman, always frail, suffered a ruptured appendix and was rushed to the hospital. Despite all medical help she did not respond and steadily grew weaker. The doctor tried to challenge her will to live by saying, "I thought you would try to be strong like John."

She replied, "John is so strong he doesn't need anyone."

That night the doctor told the farmer he didn't think his wife wanted to get well. "She's got to get well," John said, "Would another transfusion help?"

The rancher's blood proved to be the same type as his wife's, so a direct transfusion was arranged. As John lay there, his blood flowing into his wife's veins, he said, "I am going to make you well."

"Why?" she asked, eyes closed.

"Because I need you," he answered. There was a pause; then her pulse quickened, her eyes opened, and she slowly turned her head. "You never told me that before."

Writing of the incident later, the doctor said, "It wasn't the transfusion but what went with it that made the difference between life and death."

Many great love stories have been written around the theme of our deep need to be needed. Obviously, love is a two-way street where we not only give our affections but also receive similar expressions. Frustration comes when love is not returned. Some of the tenderest moments of life are when someone dear whispers, "I need you."

What is true in the human dimension is also true in the spiritual. A soul-shaking thought is that not only do we need God, but He actually needs us. It seems almost incomprehensible that the great creator could actually need us. Yet, if one reads the Bible he begins to see that the predominant theme is God's constant reaching out to His creation. This need for us was best expressed in the familiar verse, "For God so loved the world, that he gave his only begotten Son, that whosoever believeth in him should not perish, but have everlasting life" (John 3:16).

Contemplating it more deeply, the fact that God needs us does make sense. To create a being in His own image, with the ability to choose good or evil, was a great venture God undertook. Love demands reciprocal concern; therefore God gave His Son that fallen humanity could be reconciled and enter into a beautiful relation called sonship.

Scarcely had man sinned before God began building bridges to Himself for the benefit of His separated creation. First came the law; then slowly but surely the perfect plan of redemption through His Son was revealed. From Genesis through Revelation we see the insistent theme of God's so great love for us. He cannot turn His back and walk off as if we never existed.

What does this mean for us? It means, obviously, the bridge of redemption has already been built by the eternal God. It means we are assured of His forgiveness when we ask for it through His Son. It also means we can be involved with God in the joyous work of reconciling men to Himself. By sharing His plan of redemption with others we become His outreach to those still to be saved.

One's image of God will determine his eternal destiny and also his present life direction and happiness. Many view God as the eternal disciplinarian without mercy. Omar Khayyám mused:

What! out of senseless Nothing to provoke
A conscious something to resent the yoke
Of unpermitted Pleasure, under pain
Of Everlasting Penalties, if broke.

However, there is a better and more accurate view of God found in His holy Word. That image is of a God of love and justice who took our sins and put them on His Son that we might have everlasting life. It was Isaiah who mused: "Can a woman forget her sucking child, that she should not have compassion on the son of her womb? yea, they may forget, yet will I not forget thee" (49:15).

3 "This Is a Holdup!"

Suggested Scripture: Romans 2:1-11

After a rash of robberies in 1968, California's Bank of America decided to advertise pictures of thieves to assist police in capturing them. (The bank had recorded the robberies on automatic cameras and therefore had photos available.) Within a few days after the ad appeared, four out of five suspects had been spotted and apprehended. Today they are serving long sentences for their crimes.

From their unfortunate experiences with robberies, the large bank compiled interesting statistics about the crimes and criminals. They found an average bank robbery netted $1,900 and 85 percent of the thieves were caught and convicted. Robbers received an average fifteen-year sentence in federal prison for their crimes—which meant they made only about $125 per year for the dangerous endeavor. This figure is even further reduced with recovery of stolen money. It is easy to conclude that bank robbery is not a very profitable occupation, although there does not seem to be a shortage of personnel.

Some might ponder why there are so many robberies in the light of the knowledge that crime does not pay. Prisons are full of men who have planned the "perfect crime." After working as a prison chaplain, I have concluded that those participating in crimes refuse to believe they will ever be caught. The more premeditated the crime, the less the criminal expects to be apprehended. It is the same unreal optimism which makes us feel that if a common disaster hit our city and if there was only one survivor, we would be that one.

Many approach religious life and eternity with this same unreal optimism. They conjure up a white-bearded, benign God who might condemn the rest of the world—especially some races or nations—but would wink at their own simple wickedness. Yet, God's Word states plainly, "But the fearful, and unbelieving, and the abominable, and murderers, and whoremongers, and sorcerers, and idolaters, and all liars, shall have their part in the lake which burneth with fire and brimstone: which is the second death" (Rev. 21:8).

One of the clearest messages of the Bible is that of personal accountability and responsibility. Jesus talked of this constantly in His parables, and the writer of Romans emphasized, "And thinkest thou this, O man, that judgest them which do such things, and doest the same, that thou shalt escape the judgment of God?" (Rom. 2:3). Unreal optimism does nothing in the teeth of reality, and there is nothing more real than the Word of God.

Lest we despair, there is rehabilitation for the sinner. The first step is recognition of the futility of "playing the odds." Just as the criminal must really learn that crime does not pay, we must learn that sin does not pay. However, recognition is not enough. If it were, we would need only preachers and teachers to help us change. No, there must be that life-changing experience of being "born again." This is a divine work in which God gives us a new set of values, desires, and goals for our lives.

In prison we saw many paroled out with every intention of going straight. However, they had only recognized the futility of crime and had not really made a life-style change. Before long we saw them come back with new crimes added to their charge. Paul knew this frustrating cycle of recidivism: "For the good that I would I do not: but the evil which I would not, that I do" (Rom. 7:19). In despair he cries, "O wretched man that I am! who shall deliver me from the body of this death?" Then in answer he confidently replies, "I thank God through Jesus Christ our Lord" (7:24-25).

No one can explain how the divine initiative works. Yet millions have testified how their lives have been dramatically altered by the power of Jesus Christ. No longer are they living with unreal optimism or playing the odds. No longer are they slaves to their own lower nature. Now they have deep assurance and live confidently because they have accepted Christ's invitation, "Come unto me, all ye that labour and are heavy laden, and I will give you rest" (Matt. 11:28).

4 Tray Tree Temperaments

Suggested Scripture: Ephesians 3:13-21

On rocky crevices of high mountains, on perpendicular cliffs of tiny islands, on wettish bogs, and on sparcest and driest mountain slopes, some trees have lived bravely for a century or more, growing only a few feet high, straining under the pressures of hard weather. Several hundred years ago the Japanese became fascinated with these tiny trees and began the ancient art of growing bonsai—literally translated, "tray trees."

Developing forests of tray trees is no easy task. Its art, perfected in Japan, is now spreading through the Western world. The principle is simple enough. Bonsai are grown by limiting the soil and clipping the roots. By not permitting roots to dig deep in the earth through keeping the tree in a small pot, growers are able to keep the woody plant from becoming any larger than an ordinary house plant. These dwarf trees are small because they have never been permitted to expand to full potential.

Taking a look at our times, it seems as if we have a world full of bonsai men—miniature men without morals or meaning, without direction or responsibility. Our newspapers are crammed full of reports of these miniature men. The Charles Mansons heartlessly slaying innocent victims; the mad hatchet man bludgeoning at least twenty-five victims and burying their bodies in crude California graves; the miniature minded politicians rattling rockets and frightening inhabitants of this shaky and dying globe. Men, all little men, with "tray tree temperaments." T. S. Eliot well describes our age:

> . . .the hollow men
> . . .the stuffed men
> Leaning together
> Headpiece stuffed with straw!

What is so despairing is when we consider what a giant man could be. He could conquer both inner and outer space, could overcome ecological problems, could bring disease under subjection, could conquer poverty, could bring peace to flourish in the world, if only he would grow up into the man God intended him to be. God clearly tells us in His Word that the destiny of man is simply to have dominion over all the earth (Gen. 1:26). Man is also an eternal giant, destined for sharing with God the everlasting. Yet the shattering blow is that man blew all this destiny when he wilfully sinned. And we continue in that same pattern by being just as guilty as Adam with our own acts of rebellion. So instead of giants on the earth, we have a generation of bonsai men.

Lest we completely despair, God has provided a transplant from the arid and confining soil of self-indulgence to a full and free life in Him. We can be changed from "tray tree temperaments" to "giant redwoods" by a simple procedure called salvation. Paul described the experience by saying: "And I pray that Christ will be more and more at home in your hearts, living within you as you trust in him. May your roots go down deep into the soil of

God's marvelous love; and may you be able to feel and understand, as all God's children should, how long, how wide, how deep, and how high his love really is; and to experience this love for yourselves, though it is so great that you will never see the end of it or fully know or understand it. And so at last you will be filled up with God himself" (Eph. 3:17-19, The Living Bible).

Again Paul writes, "Let your roots grow down into him and draw up nourishment from him. See that you go on growing in the Lord, and become strong and vigorous in the truth" (Col. 2:7, The Living Bible).

There is only one way men become giants and that is by being transplanted from the small trays of their selfishness into the rich and free soil of God's Son, Jesus Christ. When this happens man fulfills the destiny planned for him from the beginning of creation.

5 Full Circle of Suffering

Suggested Scripture: Psalm 119:65-72

Several years ago a profound and dramatic research project began in Chicago's Billings Hospital. It was a seminar on death, in which psychiatrists, chaplains, nurses, and medical doctors studied the ultimate human crisis of facing death. It began with a request for help by Chicago theological students who asked psychiatrist Elisabeth Kubler-Ross to assist them in preparing people to accept terminal illnesses.

Dr. Ross began a research project among those who had terminal illnesses and discovered some profound lessons for living among those who are dying. Almost daily the professionals gathered behind one-way glass and observed as doctors and ministers talked with terminally ill patients. From this the professional world is beginning to change its views about how to deal with those who know they are going to die.

Basic findings of Dr. Ross and her staff is that the very ill proceed through five emotional stages on their way to death. The first stage is *denial.* Here the patient is unwilling to accept his fate and the nature of his predicament. When physical indications make denial no longer possible the patient moves into the second stage, that of *anger.* He becomes angry for no apparent reason with his doctor, his friends, his family, and the nurses. Following this comes the stage of *bargaining.* Dr.

17

Ross explained here the patient bargains to stave off the inevitable by promising to "live for God," go to church, give his body to medical science, or some other futile means. Yet, the bargaining is little more than a temporary respite in the progress toward dying.

The fourth and most difficult stage is that of *increasing depression.* The patient finally realizes what is happening to him and enters a time when he is actually grieving for his own demise. It is a trying time for both patient and loved ones. However, Dr. Ross says, this is followed by the fifth and final stage, and that is *acceptance.* Then, even though the smallest glimmer of hope will remain, he is ready to die.

An interesting note of this study was that if the patient is interrupted in any phase of this circle of suffering, he merely prolongs his agony. Therefore, Dr. Ross suggests ministers and doctors should understand these basic cycles; and rather than merely trying to cheer up the terminally ill, minister to their particular needs at that particular time.

Long before Dr. Ross and her associates began their sophisticated analysis of the dying process, Jesus made a simple but extremely sound psychological and spiritual statement: "Blessed are they that mourn; for they shall be comforted" (Matt. 5:4). To put this into context with Dr. Ross's experiments, Scripture would state: "Blessed are they who go through the full circle of suffering; for they will come to complete comfort."

While we must never deny that God has power to heal the body, we must remember we are crea-

18

tures of eternity and not just of this earth. And God heals people, not diseases. The psalmist said so eloquently, "It is good for me that I have been afflicted; that I might learn thy statutes" (119:71).

While we would desire to live in perfect health and unmitigated happiness, God at times takes us through the "valley of experience." Then, just like the terminally ill patient, we often express denial, anger, bargaining, frustration. However, if we will be patient and faithful we will find God never fails and brings us safely through to acceptance. Two Scripture verses keep ringing in our hearts: "And we know that all things work together for good to them that love God, to them who are the called according to his purpose" (Rom. 8:28). Add to this: "When thou passest through the waters, I will be with thee; and through the rivers, they shall not overflow thee: when thou walkest through the fire, thou shalt not be burned; neither shall the flame kindle upon thee" (Isa. 43:2).

6 Decisive Living

Suggested Scripture: Matthew 6:24-34

A scene from the dramatic story of Gen. Curtis Lemay finds the famed military leader in an old flying boxcar, carelessly puffing on a cigar. A young officer, fresh from training school, angrily approaches another junior officer to complain bitterly, "What's the matter with that old fool? Doesn't he know the aircraft is a firetrap? With him smoking, this plane could blow up." To this the officer calmly replied, "It wouldn't dare."

In our age of many weak-willed men it is refreshing to find decisive people. Thus, stories of Lemay and General Patton find a ready audience. A world is seeking someone who stands sure. This accounts for much of the success of Billy Graham and General Booth. While the masses preach "situational ethics" and "follow your feelings," some men stand like cliffs against the raging tide. They are decisive and dramatic, never wavering in the wind of change.

Artists have softened the lines of Christ's face until some see Him as weak-willed and perhaps a little effeminate. However, this picture is wholly false. Each portrait of Christ found in Scripture is one with the strength of steel, with His face set like a flint. He was not crucified for saying, "Consider the lilies, how they grow," but for implying, "Consider the thieves, how they steal." Many of our frustrations would go if we had the same spiritual determination as Christ.

20

Paul, about to die, leaves practical advice to young Timothy: "Turn your back on the turbulent desires of youth and give your positive attention to goodness, faith, love and peace in company with those who approach God in sincerity" (II Tim. 2:22). As one humorist observed, most of us do not flee temptation, we merely crawl away, hoping it will overcome us. Our lack of decisive action keeps us in defeat.

After fourteen fear-filled days in turbulent waters, the tiny ship carrying Paul and his party crashed on the rocks of Malta. Some swam for shore and others struggled for land by grabbing broken bits of the wooden ship. All finally made it, and stood around shivering in the cold while prisoner Paul gathered sticks to build a fire. Suddenly, a poisonous snake leaped from the wood and sank its fangs into the apostle's arm, "And when the barbarians saw the venomous beast hang on his hand, they said among themselves, No doubt this man is a murderer, whom, though he hath escaped the sea, yet vengeance suffereth not to live" (Acts 28:4). But the Bible notes, "And he shook off the beast into the fire, and felt no harm" (28:5). Here is a lesson for us to utterly reject that venomous asp that would destroy our souls.

Some try to come to Christ, yet feel frustrated. The cause is simple. To gain the new life, one must shed the old. Christ reminded His listeners that one cannot put new wine into old bottles, nor can he sew new cloth on old material. His salvation is not an appendage to his present life; rather, it is a new garment. This means we must reject the old

21

to find the new. It means absolute rejection of all we once held dear. Christ does not come to be a part of our life, He comes to *be* our life.

Many want the best of two worlds. They wish to be religious enough for God to be within hearing distance but far enough away not to interfere with their worldly involvement. Tragically, these are very frustrated people because they refuse to recognize, as Jesus said, "Ye cannot serve God and mammon" (Luke 16:13). Decisive action is needed, with utter rejection of evil as well as total involvement in Christ's kingdom.

The world is rushing toward Armageddon, where no one sits on the fence. In our age of ulcers and aspirin, of rocket rattling and escapism through self-explosion, we can be decisive men with steel in us if we turn to Christ. We need not be ruled by our own lower natures because Christ can make us free. All we must do is present ourselves to Him and He begins the tempering process (see Rom. 12:1).

7 How to Catch a Monkey

Suggested Scripture: Psalm 77

One of the oldest methods of catching monkeys is so simple that one would doubt it works if there was not so much evidence to the contrary. A hunter merely cuts a small hole in a gourd, ties it to a post or tree, and then places seeds in the hollowed-out gourd.

Before long a monkey comes by and, overwhelmed by curiosity, reaches through the tiny hole to explore the gourd's contents. Feeling the seeds, he scoops them up in his hand and tries to pull his fist through the tiny hole. To his dismay, he finds he cannot free himself. Because he does not want to let go of his precious treasure, he keeps his fist closed until captors come. He could be free if only he had learned to let go.

In some of our actions we too are as foolish as the monkey. It is true some hold onto possessions until they are caught in the frustration of materialism. Others hold onto their tiny seeds of pleasure until sin swallows them up in rapid fury. Tragically, there are even some Christians who hold onto their self-pity until they are captured by total confusion.

Sometimes we come to the altar with our problems and frustrations clutched in our frail hands. While we carry them to God, we refuse to let go of them. We fret to God about our needs, complain a little, and wonder why the heavens are brass and God so far away. Doesn't He care? Is anyone really there?

Regardless of how alone we feel at times like this, many others have stood in the same place. In Psalm 77 Asaph complains to God, "In the day of my trouble I sought the Lord: my sore ran in the night, and ceased not." Then he moves on to express many of our own woes, "My soul refused to be comforted." He even admits, "I remembered God, and was troubled: I complained, and my spirit was overwhelmed." In bitterness he pleads, "Will the Lord cast off for ever? Doth his promise fail for evermore? Hath God forgotten to be gracious? hath he in anger shut up his tender mercies?" (vv. 2-3, 7-9).

Then, moving from that trying experience, he gives the key to becoming free from frustration: "And I said, This is my infirmity: but I will remember the years of the right hand of the most High" (v. 10). When he let go of his self-pity and began praising God for past faithfulness, he was finally set free.

We often pray about matters and in our frustration ponder God. Like the psalmist, we become troubled; for who can understand the infinite and eternal God! To try to understand His beginning, His being, His majesty merely causes a cold wind of fear to blow about our troubled heads. We are too much bound to earth to comprehend the everlasting. However, when we, like the psalmist, begin to review His personal part in creation, how He has always been actively involved in mankind, how He has ever been a present help in trouble, we then let go of our self-pity and are set free. No wonder the psalmist said, "I will meditate also of all thy work, and talk of thy doings" (v. 12).

Jesus simply said, "What things soever ye desire, when ye pray, believe that ye receive them, and ye shall have them" (Mark 11:24). This is real faith: dropping the seeds of our doubts, our frustrations, our self-pity, and letting go to let God have His way. When we remember His faithfulness and care throughout ages past, we are assured He is more than aware of our present.

8 Only an Onesiphorus

Suggested Scripture: II Timothy 1:13-18

While some men paint the face of history with dramatic and colorful lives, there are others who change its direction through quiet but powerful influence. Felix Kersten was such a man.

During those blood-filled days between 1940 and 1945 when names like Hitler, Himmler, and Goering struck terror in the hearts of millions, Dr. Kersten rescued thousands from sure death at the hands of the mad-dog Nazis. As personal physician and manual therapist to Heinrich Himmler, he had amazing powers over Germany's number two man. Dr. Kersten used this influence to keep many from becoming victims of the wanton killers who led Germany.

Week by week Kersten snatched Himmler's victims from concentration camps and gas chambers. The World Jewish Council credits him with saving 60,000 of their people, and the number of Dutch, Poles, Finns, and Norwegians he saved is difficult to estimate. The absorbing story of Dr. Kersten's mission is told in the best seller *The Man with the Miraculous Hands.* The great influence of this little-known and quiet man changed the course of destiny for many, and perhaps for the whole world.

While all recognize the impact of famous men, we too often little understand the dynamics of quiet lives hidden from headlines and bright lights of publicity. Thomas Gray wisely observed:

26

Full many a gem of purest ray serene
　　The dark unfathomed caves of ocean bear:
Full many a flower is born to blush unseen,
　　And waste its sweetness on the desert air.

Paul the apostle is familiar to almost every inhabitant of the free world, certainly to every Christian. Yet this great man of God frankly admits his life had been influenced and possibly even changed by a little-known Christian named Onesiphorus. Of him Paul writes: "The Lord give mercy unto the house of Onesiphorus; for he oft refreshed me, and was not ashamed of my chain: But, when he was in Rome, he sought me out very diligently, and found me. The Lord grant unto him that he may find mercy of the Lord in that day: and in how many things he ministered unto me at Ephesus, thou knowest very well" (II Tim. 1:16-18).

In this last note that Paul would write before his execution, the great apostle speaks with warmth toward Onesiphorus because of his courage, faithfulness, and love. Other Christians had deserted Paul in a time of crisis, but Onesiphorus risked capture and ridicule to seek out Paul and encourage him. It might have been this influence that helped Paul go to his grave unafraid and with the assurance he had fought a good fight and kept the faith.

All of us have had the joy of people touching our lives in times of crisis. To have someone simply say, "I'm praying for you" in times of trial can often lift our hearts from deep depression. To simply know God sends an Onesiphorus along to let us know someone cares can be joy to a weary soul. Such people with this kind of influence have great impact on our destiny.

One great Christian who feels she has no speaking ability and little to offer in terms of talent simply writes letters of encouragement to those in need. Testimonies of the impact of this generous act of love indicate she too is an Onesiphorus.

Probably all of us would like to be of great reputation with much accomplished for God. Some of us recognize we might not be able to do what some others can do for God. Yet all of us can be loving persons of compassion to lift a discouraged brother. And Jesus notes, "Inasmuch as ye have done it unto one of the least of these my brethren, ye have done it unto me" (Matt. 25:40).

9 Flooded Reservoirs

Suggested Scripture: Mark 7:14-23

Twenty million tons of raging water roared down the mountain, ripping trees, crushing cabins, hurling humans high only to suck them to a watery death. On that tragic afternoon more than two thousand people perished as the placid valley village of Johnstown, Pennsylvania, was nearly washed into oblivion. Lake Conemaugh's dam had burst in the iron-rich Alleghenies, forever marking May 31, 1889, as a day of death.

Piecing together causes of the tragedy, officials concluded the flawed earth dam had burst as rainstorms drove waters high. The swollen waters spilled over with erosion, cutting deeper and deeper until finally the deep dam exploded outward, belching walls of water seventy feet high. Trains were tossed from tracks, houses skewed by trees, buildings crumbled, and people screamed to their deaths while being swallowed by the angry black waters. The Johnstown flood was forever etched deep in the memory of man.

Floods are almost always destructive and dams are susceptible to breaking. For this reason valley authorities have been established and rigid codes set, controlling structure of water barriers. Men work long and hard hours to prevent another Johnstown tragedy.

Our lives are reservoirs of emotions, desires, and passions dammed up by our will. These reservoirs are being flooded constantly with our thoughts, driving passions high, often eroding conscience with sin that breaks forth in rapid fury, destructive in force, and tragic in consequence. Our overt evil actions are merely spilled-over thoughts of the heart. God's Word declares, "As he thinketh in his heart, so is he" (Prov. 23:7).

What is true in the negative is also true in the positive. If our thoughts are pure and Christ-centered, these will drive our compassionate emotions high and spill over in good to mankind. These emotions are carefully controlled by the Holy Spirit and so do not erode conscience or will. Rather, they are useful in energy and most constructive for the total good of mankind. This Christ-controlled temperament is like a mighty river channeled for greatest good.

Overt actions are merely extensions or actualizations of inner thoughts. Jesus talked of this when He noted, "That which cometh out of the man, that defileth the man. For from within, out of the heart of men, proceed evil thoughts, adulteries, fornications, murders, thefts, covetousness, wickedness, deceit, lasciviousness, an evil eye, blasphemy, pride, foolishness: All these evil things come from within, and defile the man" (Mark 7:20-23).

Because sin's origin is in the heart, Jesus could rightly say, "Whosoever looketh on a woman to lust after her hath committed adultery with her already in his heart" (Matt. 5:28). Add the words of Proverbs: "Keep thy heart with all diligence; for out of it are the issues of life" (4:23). Then James, in a very practical manner, notes a build-up of bad thoughts erupting into evil action: "But every man is tempted, when he is drawn away of his own lust, and enticed. Then when lust hath conceived, it bringeth forth sin: and sin, when it is finished, bringeth forth death" (James 1:14-15).

Therefore, the touchstone of effective living is a proper thought life. If we flood our reservoirs with evil, lustful, and negative thoughts, our lives will reflect that decision. On the other hand, if we flood our hearts with proper, holy, and righteous thoughts, we reap the fruit of that effort. Paul is careful to admonish young Christians: "Finally, brethren, whatsoever things are true, whatsoever things are honest, whatsoever things are just, whatsoever things are pure, whatsoever things are lovely, whatsoever things are of good report; if there be any virtue, and if there be any praise, think on these things" (Phil. 4:8).

10 First Place for Prayer

Suggested Scripture: I Timothy 2:1-8

While conducting a private prayer meeting for men, a pastor was suddenly inspired to ask prayer for a well-known former church leader who had denied the faith and ventured into the occult. Upon making request, the pastor noted that one young man became highly agitated and refused to join in the prayer.

Some time later the pastor was approached by that same young man who asked, "Pastor, please forgive me. When you asked prayer for that church leader I became so angry because it is false prophets like him who cause so much evil in the world. My parents are not Christians today just because of this man."

To this the wise pastor stated, "While I can appreciate your feelings, still we must be obedient to God." Then he showed the youth Paul's letter to Timothy: "I exhort therefore, that first of all, supplications, prayers, intercessions, and giving of thanks, be made for all men; For kings, and for all that are in authority" (I Tim. 2:1, 2). Then the preacher asked, "Have you ever prayed for this theologian?" The young man bowed his head and stated he had never prayed for him. To which the pastor added kindly, "Only after we are obedient in prayer can we then move on to criticism."

In our age of shouting militants, angry pickets, and raging radicals, there is a tendency for us to criticize freely but carry through with very little personal responsibility. Paul clearly states our priority should be first to pray about people and things before venturing comments or criticisms. Only after prayer can righteous decisions and evaluations be made.

Prayer, to most active Americans, seems so passive. Yet if we are truly obedient we will make it a priority. We should never underestimate its power. In his touching book *Christ in the Communist Prisons* Richard Wurmbrand relates how the leader of his country was saved because thousands of Christians prayed for him. After many years of avowed communism, Prime Minister Gheoghiu-Dej of Rumania returned to the faith of his mother. He had been converted through a maidservant in his home. Christianity gave him the strength to defy his Soviet masters and ignore their threats, and consequently he opened new relations with the West. In doing so, many religious prisoners were released and returned to their families.

God desires we give priority to prayer because, as Paul notes, "For this is good and acceptable in the sight of God our Saviour; Who will have all men to be saved, and to come unto the knowledge of the truth" (I Tim. 2:3, 4). Perhaps we would be selective in who is saved, but God loves all men and we fulfill His will when we pray they may come to a knowledge of the truth.

Sometimes we despair, wondering if God will answer our prayers. Habakkuk had this frustration and asked God about it, He received this reply: "But these things I plan won't happen right away.

Slowly, steadily, surely, the time approaches when the vision will be fulfilled. If it seems slow, do not despair, for these things will surely come to pass. Just be patient! They will not be overdue a single day!" (2:3, The Living Bible).

11 Man Starves to Feed Birds

Suggested Scripture: Matthew 7:7-11

Los Angeles residents were shocked and saddened recently to learn one of their own was starving himself just to feed the birds in two city parks. Newspaper reporters learned of the strange story and reported it nationally. Retired Raymond Lopez, eighty years old, gaunt, sick, and feeble, explained, "I don't care about myself anymore. I'm only interested in helping all things that suffer and all things that are hungry."

Most of Lopez's social security check and pension goes to pay the delivery man who comes every Tuesday with 2,800 pounds of feed for his feathered friends. The bill is about $150 a week. While friends have encouraged Lopez to take a trip, relax, or enjoy material things, he merely replies, "I'd rather go hungry myself than let my birds go hungry."

While most would question the wisdom of the bird lover's action, still the elderly California gentleman has learned one valuable lesson of life. That is, it is indeed more blessed to give than receive. The world is really divided into only two camps—the givers and the getters. More eloquently phrased, they could be called the eternalist and the materialist. Jesus talked much of the two attitudes, and firmly positions Himself and His followers in the camp of the givers.

While people call Darwin's *Survival of the Fittest* an evolutionary theory, it could more correctly be called a philosophy of life. The getter is one who believes he must take all, even from the weak and dying. He seems to fare well until another comes along stronger than he or until age crushes his strength and puts him on the mercy of others. On the other hand, the eternalist believes in ultimate accountability before God and knows he is placed on earth not as a taker but as one who helps, gives, loves, and aids. While it is true that most of the world laughs at the giver, still he is the only one who endures. He has placed treasures where earth's fickle circumstances cannot touch them.

This is a cruel and evil world. God gives us a choice to position ourselves in which camp we wish to dwell. We can be part of the problem or we can be part of the solution. We can be filled with racism, hatred, animosity. We can ignore the hurts of humanity and close our eyes to our responsibilities. We can close our eyes, hearts, and hands to the needs of others and greedily grasp all we can. Conversely, we can give ourselves to God, whose nature is to give. We can be involved in redeeming mankind to Himself. And deep within every man is that God-given desire to give.

However, it must be understood that the gift is as important as the attitude of giving. Giving must have direction if it is therapeutic. To truly help the hungry of the world we need to give the Bread of Life, Jesus Christ. To merely give food to the starving without Christ at best staves off ultimate death. But to give Christ assures of eternal life and ministers to physical needs as well. God's greatest gift was not fields of wheat or hills dotted with cattle. Rather, His greatest gift was that of His Son who makes all things right. Jesus simply stated our priority by noting, "Seek ye first the kingdom of God, and his righteousness; and all these things shall be added unto you" (Matt. 6:33).

May our giving have direction. Jesus said, "What man is there of you, who if his son ask bread, will he give him a stone? Or if he ask a fish, will he give him a serpent?" (Matt. 7:9, 10). Ben Franklin mused, "He who shall introduce into public affairs the principles of primitive Christianity will change the face of the world."

12 Notes on Names

Suggested Scripture: Isaiah 9:1-7

Until about the year 1100, most people in Europe had only one name. With population increasing it became difficult to distinguish among people, so surnames were added. These came from four primary sources: a man's *occupation,* such as John Cook, or Miller; *location,* such as John Overhill or Brook; *patronymical,* such as John's son (Johnson); and *characteristics,* such as John Small, Short, Longfellow, and so forth.

In addition to need for identification, one occupation had to go a step further: the fighting men. In the Middle Ages combatants wore heavy suits of armor which made them unrecognizable. To prevent friend from fighting friend, each knight identified himself by painting a colorful design on his armor. In this manner was born the family coat of arms.

Today there is a revival of interest in origins of family names. Companies offering to research the family coat of arms are flourishing. Some psychologists see in this a rebellion against our impersonal society that has reduced the individual to a series of numbers stored somewhere in a computer.

God, who gave man his first name, obviously felt names to be important. Through Isaiah He speaks of His coming Son: "And his name shall be called Wonderful, Counsellor, The mighty God, The everlasting Father, The Prince of· Peace" (9:6). By careful study the scholar finds each of Christ's names most significant and tells us much about our Lord.

Wonderful denotes the enchantment of His earthly birth, life, death, and resurrection. Millions of other babies have been born in even more abject poverty than Christ; yet what makes the difference in His birth is not its lowliness but its highness. His divinity is that magic of Christmas demanding attention of a rude and restless world.

Counsellor suggests a friend who gives guidance. Henry Ford observed, "My best friend is he who brings out the best in me." Christ, as counsellor in crisis, has far more expertise than psychologist or psychiatrist for leading, guiding, and directing our lives.

The mighty God. Artists and poets are loved because they are able to put into paintings and words what we all have felt at times. Christ also is loved because He was the articulation of God. As the Word observes, "For in him dwelleth all the fulness of the Godhead bodily" (Col. 2:9).

The everlasting Father denotes personal care and protection. We can tell our heavenly Father things we never dare tell another with assurance. He still loves and cares for us. A Father knows us and still loves. He protects, and enjoys His children.

The Prince of Peace tells of the rightness Christ brings into a life. In the midst of a world of turmoil, Christ gives peace because He is constantly with His children. And one day peace will come for all mankind when the Prince of Peace reigns forever and ever.

Names are important and mean much to we who

own them. However, for those who know Christ there is a far more important name than our earthly one. God promises to those who are faithful He will give a white stone of approval and "in the stone a new name written, which no man knoweth saving he that receiveth it" (Rev. 2:17). And as Christ admonished, "Rejoice, because your names are written in heaven" (Luke 10:20).

13 Deceptive Pillars

Suggested Scripture: I Peter 2:1-10

Famed English architect Sir Christopher Wren designed a large church dome so unique that he became the object of jealous criticism among his colleagues. During the construction they created such a stir that the authorities demanded Wren add two huge supporting pillars to keep it from collapsing. Wren bitterly objected, insisting on the strength of his structure and the wisdom of his new architectural innovation. Nevertheless opposition prevailed and the pillars were added.

Fifty years passed and the dome needed repainting. When workers began, they discovered that the two added pillars did not even touch the roof. They were short by two feet each. Wren had confidence in his work. The authorities, during his lifetime, saw the pillars, assumed they reached the roof and the controversy died. They felt secure although the pillars were free standing and supported nothing.

Man has built many pillars to support his little world and to keep things from falling in on him. Often these pillars seem strong and able to stand stress, but many times are just as useless as Wren's fake columns. Some have constructed pillars of religion, beautiful in structure, and certainly they seem strong enough. However, religion is meaningless without the Person of Jesus Christ who plainly states, "I am the way, the truth, and the life: no man cometh unto the Father, but by me" (John

14:6). Pillars of religion are free standing without Christ and have no hold on eternity.

Others proudly build pillars of intellectualism, resting in their own mental prowess while rejecting God and His Son, Christ. Thomas Paine was such a man. He disclaimed any belief in God, saying in essence he was the master of his own fate, the captain of his own soul. However, at death he cried, "I'm lost, I'm lost, I'm lost."

Lord Byron, the romantic poet and idol of the court ladies in the last century, built pillars of pleasure. He abandoned any sense of responsibility, saying in essence, "Eat, drink, be merry; for this is what life is all about." However, his pillars were also free standing; for on his last birthday, at age 36, he moaned, "The flowers and fruits of life are gone; the worm, the canker, and the grief are mine alone."

Just like the building authorities of Wren's time, we can be easily deceived by structures of philosophies. The Bible warns, "There is a way which seemeth right unto a man, but the end thereof are the ways of death" (Prov. 14:12). Sturdy as they might seem, pillars of pleasure, intellectualism, and mere religion do not keep enemies such as fear, frustration, and confusion from smashing during hours of blackest crisis.

Lest we despair, there is a structure ample for the pressing vicissitudes of life and the ultimate crisis of death. Peter talked of this in his letter to early Christians: "Come to Christ, who is the living Foundation of Rock upon which God builds; though men have spurned him, he is very precious to God who had chosen him above all others. . . . As Scripture expresses it, 'See, I am sending Christ to be the carefully chosen, precious Cornerstone of my church, and I will never disappoint those who trust in him'" (I Peter 2:4, 6, The Living Bible). As Wren had confidence in his architectural creation, so Peter has perfect confidence in the structure God builds. He realizes that pillars of men are totally unnecessary. Only if Christ designs the life will it stand, and if Christ does not design it all the pillars in the world cannot hold it up.

> My hope is built on nothing less
> > Than Jesus' blood and righteousness;
> I dare not trust the sweetest frame,
> > But wholly lean on Jesus' name.

14 Bramble Bush King

Suggested Scripture: Judges 9:1-21

Even in his lifetime many anecdotes and wise sayings were attributed to Lincoln, which in reality were words from another. Probably no other American has been quoted more than this great president. One of his wisest sayings is that we get the leadership we deserve. Three thousand years earlier, Israel had learned the tragic truth of this statement.

God's man Gideon had died after a valiant life. He had left behind a rich spiritual heritage and seventy-two sons to carry on the work he had started. However, when he died so did Israel's spiritual life; consequently there was a void in noble leadership. None of his seventy-one legitimate sons wanted to take the strong stand Gideon had, so there was a transitory period with little or no leadership.

In this void, Abimelech, a son by a Shechem concubine, bribed fellow countrymen until they made him their leader. His pitch was, "Isn't it better to have one leader than seventy?" Disaster followed.

His first official act after gaining power was to order the massacre of his half-brothers. Seventy were killed and only the youngest, Jotham, escaped. Immediately the land was plunged into chaos, with murder and intrigue the order of the day. So great was the sorrow that people rued the day they had selected Abimelech. The surviving

44

brother, Jotham, then stands on Mount Gerizim to speak a parable.

In the parable Israel went out to choose a ruler. First, they went to the olive tree, which represented richness. The olive said it could not lead them because this would mean leaving his fatness and wealth. Next, they approached the fig tree, which responded negatively, saying it could not leave its sweetness and good fruit to rule Israel. Then the approach is made to the vine, which responds similarly that it cannot leave its wine which cheers both God and man. Finally, the offer is made to the bramble or weed, which immediately accepts. The parable is ended by saying a devouring fire will come out of the bramble. And, it did.

The lesson is clear and concise. We must accept responsibility or evil will prevail. Creation is incomplete, for in the beginning God ordained man to "replenish the earth, and subdue it" (Gen. 1:28). Satan understands our God-given task and would divert us with our own pleasure and desire. Because many have been diverted, we have reaped a world of hatred, prejudice, war, anxiety, and fear. God never intended it to be so, and, it can be different if we live responsibly and righteously.

Often we are tempted to feel so small and inadequate for the task. We see so much evil, so much hatred and animosity. However, Christ desires we start where we are with what we have. We must understand the world is a garden to be cultivated, not a playground to be frolicked in.

There will never be a void of leadership. If we default, the Hitlers and Stalins, and other crude, crass, and evil leaders that have plunged our world into chaos are there to take over. But as we accept our responsibility and present our "bodies a living sacrifice, holy, acceptable unto God, which is [our] reasonable service" (Rom.12:1), then peace prevails and good comes.

The wicked have had the world too long. Our personal world and the larger world of mankind will be much different if we but let Christ live and rule through us. Like the songwriter, may we pray:

> Millions now in sin and shame are dying;
>> Listen to their sad and bitter cry;
> Hasten, brother, hasten to the rescue;
>> Quickly answer, "Master, here am I."

15 Making of the Mafia

Suggested Scripture: Romans 12:1-21

For nearly seven hundred years the Mafia has struck terror in the hearts of its victims. Recent books like *Honor Thy Father* and *The Godfather* have exposed the brutality of this organized group of thugs sometimes known as "Costra Nostra," or the "Black Hand." Where there is much speculation about the Mafia's origin, most historians agree on the Monday, 1242, when a French soldier viciously attacked a young Palermo maid on her wedding day. As word spread through the island, a band of Sicilians retaliated by butchering a French troop. Historians think the Mafia began at this point, taking its name from the anguished cry of the girl's mother running through the streets shouting, *"Ma fia, ma fia"* ("my daughter, my daughter").

While parts of this incident may be highly romanticized or exaggerated, there is no doubt that an organized resistance group arose at that time, Later it became known throughout the world as the Mafia. What may have started as an attempt to right a great wrong has evolved into a loathsome parasite on society dealing in extortion, murder, kidnapping, prostitution, and drugs. Great efforts are underway to rid society of this blight, but the task seems almost impossible.

Vengeance, however justified it might seem at the time, always ends destroying the one who wields it. Revolutionary governments who seek to

47

get even by overthrow, intrigue, and murder, most often end up being the oppressor. And no one can oppress like one who has been oppressed. Getting even merely starts the circle of vengeance which keeps enlarging until total destruction comes. As a prison chaplain, I saw four men murdered in one year and each killing was over something very small. People were on the getting-even syndrome until death was the outcome.

There is one eternal reason why man cannot successfully wield the weapon of vengeance. That is because it is reserved for God alone. Paul mused, "Dearly beloved, avenge not yourselves, but rather give place unto wrath: for it is written, Vengeance is mine; I will repay, saith the Lord" (Rom. 12:19). While man can see only the exterior, God sees each man's heart and therefore can more wisely deal with motives and actions. We do not have all the facts at our disposal, while God, who created each man, knows all mitigating circumstances and can rightly judge each heart.

Many times we thrill at the great battle victories we read about in the Bible. It does show God's guidance and care in these circumstances. But what a different Bible we might have if Israel had learned the lesson of letting God take care of all their enemies and oppressors. Did not God say, "The Lord shall fight for you, and ye shall hold your peace" (Exod. 14:14)? And again, "The Lord your God which goeth before you, he shall fight for you, according to all that he did for you in Egypt before your eyes" (Deut. 1:30). Was this promise not fulfilled several times in Israel's history? It happened once at the Red Sea under Moses, another time with the threatening tribe of Sennacherib, and again when God opened Elisha's servant's eyes to the host of angels encamped about.

Whatever our speculation, one thing is certain: on a personal level we do not have the right to get even or pay back a wrong. Christ gave a higher law of returning good for evil, love for hate, blessing for cursing. To do this calls for strength greater than that of getting even. Anyone can start the circle of vengeance, prejudice, bitterness, and anger. But the true child of God will trust his Father enough to let God take care of not only him but also those who wish to position themselves as enemies.

16 The Armless Soldier

Suggested Scripture: Matthew 7:1-8

Napoleon had a genius in igniting the common man to fevered patriotism. In doing this he often told this story: Once, while visiting a province he came on an old soldier with one arm severed, dressed in full uniform. On his uniform the proud fighter displayed the coveted Legion of Honor. "Where did you lose your arm?" Napoleon asked.

"At Austerlitz, sire," came the soldier's brisk reply.

"And for that you received the Legion of Honor?"

"Yes, sire. It is but a small token to pay for the decoration."

"You must be," the emperor said, "the kind of man who regrets he did not lose both arms for his country."

"What then would have been my reward?" asked the one-armed man.

"Then," Napoleon replied, "I would have awarded you a *double* Legion of Honor." With that the proud old fighter drew his sword and immediately cut off his other arm.

This story was circulated for years and believed without question until one day someone asked, "How?"

Often we accept without question what people tell us, never stopping to think things through or even doubt the wisdom of the words. Not long ago *Reader's Digest* reported the arrest of a man who had collected thousands of dollars for the mother of the "unknown soldier." These illustrations prove P.T. Barnum's cynical assertion that a sucker is born every minute.

Tragically, willingness to accept anything without question spills over into the very serious and eternal issue of religion. There are many who willingly accept what others say about the Bible without ever once opening its pages to check for themselves. Some of the church's most severe critics are those who never bother to enter church doors and find out what is going on. And, the most vocal enemies of Christ are many times those who have never really read about His life in the Gospels, but have received their information through very faulty filters of people's prejudice.

God's Word speaks clearly about our personal responsibility in learning about Him. "Work out your own salvation with fear and trembling" (Phil. 2:12). Again Paul writes, "Study to show thyself approved unto God, a workman that needeth not to be ashamed, rightly dividing the word of truth" (II Tim. 2:15).

It has been wisely remarked that God has no grandchildren. This means we cannot inherit our relationship with God through parents, but individually must make commitments to Christ. It could also be added that religion cannot be by osmosis. We cannot absorb righteousness through indirect measures, such as by talking with someone who knows God as his heavenly Father. Often we are like cartoonist Charles Schultz's character who comments, "I was an authority on the Book of

51

Revelation until one day I met someone who had read it."

Jesus rightly answered critics trying to trick Him with religious sophistry, "Ye do err, not knowing the scriptures, nor the power of God" (Matt. 22:29). Sadly, we have grown into a generation who have philosophies about and opinions on Scripture but seldom read to know what God's Word says. This is indeed the day the prophet saw when there would be a famine of the Word of God in the land.

There is an interesting proverb that simply states, "He that answereth a matter before he heareth it, it is folly and shame unto him" (18:13). God's Word does speak on the great issues of life. The mysterious questions of good and evil, of why there is illness and war, the answers to our spiritual and earthly dilemmas are all in the Word. But each must seek the answer for himself. Our relationship with Christ must be on a first-name basis.

17 The Great Piltdown Hoax

Suggested Scripture: I Corinthians 13

For more than forty years the Piltdown man was an honored member of the society of "earliest humans." Then a startling discovery proved him to be an enormous fraud. The story of the fascinating and diabolical plot to deceive has recently been told in *The Piltdown Forgery* by famed anthropologist J. S. Weiner.

In early 1912 fossil hunter Charles Dawson brought the first finds of the Piltdown man to the British Museum. Immediately the finder became famous, and soon other fragments of the "Missing link" began coming in from Dawson. The find was even named "Eoanthropus dawsoni—Dawson's Dawn Man." However, forty years later scientists found that Dawson had deceived them. The jaw had come from a modern ape, with the faker "fossilizing" it by staining it mahogany with iron salt and bichromate. An oil paint, probably red sienna, had stained the chewing surfaces of the teeth. Further tests revealed every fragment of the Piltdown a forgery. It was probably the greatest hoax perpetrated on the scientific community in history.

While motivations for deception vary, still the drive to deceive is very much part of our society. The greatest deceiver of all, Satan, disguises himself as an angel of light, moving and motivating many to perpetrate hoaxes—which, incidentally, are almost always exposed. One of the most subtle deceptions ever played on man by Satan has been the rearrangement of words which at first might seem reasonable but in reality are destructive and demeaning. The Bible says, "God is love." Satan has convinced the world to rearrange that statement to read, "Love is God."

Because this hoax has been perpetrated, many acts of violence, indecency, and immorality have been committed in the name of love. Sexual infidelity can be justified if indeed love is God. Self-explosion in excess and perverted behavior can get acceptance if we reverse the words of this simple truth. However, reversing these words carries the same reasoning as to say, "If one ship can cross the ocean in six days, then six ships can cross the ocean in one day."

Because love can be abused and misinterpreted, Paul the apostle spent much time defining this emotion and action. He simply says:

> This love of which I speak is slow to lose patience—it looks for a way of being constructive. It is not possessive: it is neither anxious to impress nor does it cherish inflated ideas of its own importance. Love has good manners and does not pursue selfish advantage. It is not touchy. It does not compile statistics of evil or gloat over the wickedness of other people. On the contrary it is glad with all good men when truth prevails. Love knows no limit to its endurance, no end to its trust, no fading of its hope: it can outlast anything. It is, in fact, the one thing that still stands when all else has fallen.—I Cor. 13, Phillips.

Love that is real is righteous, clean, and pure because God is love.

Marriages and lives have been ruined because

men and women placed their values on a deceptive philosophy of love. Often they have followed their feelings and flesh, only to have the bitter taste of wormwood linger long in their mouths after the fire of passion dies.

Daily we are bombarded with the insidious hoax, "Love is God." We see it in every magazine and newspaper. We hear it in every silly song blaring from our transistors. We see it in every television sequence; and our world of broken homes, alcoholics, and drug-dazed youth are tragic testimony that the doctrine is coming through. It is time someone exposed the hoax for what it is, and by example and testimony refuted the insidious deception destroying our society and our souls. Jesus talked of our time when He declared, "For as in the days that were before the flood they were eating and drinking, marrying and giving in marriage, until the day that Noah entered into the ark, And knew not until the flood came, and took them all away; so shall also the coming of the Son of man be" (Matt 24:38-39). Love is not God. God is love, and the world cannot survive on any other philosophy.

18 The Song and the Sea Monster

Suggested Scripture: Psalm 40:2-8

An old Indian legend tells how Teko, the dread sea monster, was defeated by the strength of a song. Young Indian Brave Kewets wanted to marry the maiden Weyona, but her grandmother would not consent unless Teko was captured and brought to her. Bravely Kewets lured the sea monster to a shallow stream and sank his harpoon deep. But as soon as the harpoon hit, the giant monster began thrashing about, dragging Kewets into the foaming water. The young brave, according to the tale, was about to perish when the mythical bird Kingfisher appeared overhead.

Kingfisher flew low, instructing Kewets to sing a song with him from the Pleiades: "You shall not have my harpoon. Shall not kill me, eat me. I am too dangerously strong. Stronger than any Teko." Together they sang this song; and legend says that so intense was the song's strength, Kewets was able to capture the sea monster. Teko was taken to the grandmother and a wedding ceremony followed.

Indians were among the first to recognize the tremendous impact of music. Today's prophets, seers, and evangelists are often musicians. Tragically, many of them deliver doctrines of despair and depravity through much of their music. And the message seems to be getting through. Most of today's music reflects a sickness in our society. Sensualism, materialism, and hopelessness are reflected; and the message is, "Eat, drink, and be merry for tomorrow we die." Many people are becoming alarmed at what is being communicated, feeling that several generations to come will suffer shock waves of this doctrine of despair.

While the picture of our society is sordid, there is a glorious hope. The psalmist said, "He brought me up also out of an horrible pit, out of the miry clay, and set my feet upon a rock, and established my goings. And he hath put a new song in my mouth" (40:2, 3). That is a musical doctrine that makes sense and is far from the songs of lamentation this world knows. It is a song with power to give meaning to all of life. This new song is of salvation through Christ and how our despairing existence can change through an encounter with Him. It teaches responsibility and accountability. It is indeed a song of strength, giving us power over any monster of sin or evil.

But if this new song is to be effective we must sing it with a meaning that is life changing. Ezekiel talked of those who merely listened for entertainment by quoting God:

> Son of dust, your people are whispering behind your back. They talk about you in their houses and whisper about you at the doors, saying, "Come on, let's have some fun! Let's go hear him tell us what the Lord is saying!" So they come as though they are sincere and sit before you listening. But they have no intention of doing what I tell them to; they talk very sweetly about loving the Lord, but with their hearts they are loving their money. You are very entertaining to them, like someone who sings lovely songs with a beautiful voice or plays well on an instrument. They hear what you say but don't pay any attention to it!—Ezek. 33:30-32, The Living Bible

There is a new song Christ gives, but it must be accepted with sincerity of repentance and restoration. God's Word says: "If my people, which are called by my name, shall humble themselves, and pray, and seek my face, and turn from their wicked ways; then will I hear from heaven, and will forgive their sin, and will heal their land" (II Chron. 7:14). The new song is not filled with sound and fury like the lyrics of the world. Rather, it is an overbubbling joy of spirit Christ gives to those who believe on Him. His song of strength will not just carry us through the many problems of life, but will make us dynamic conquerors through Christ. No wonder the redeemed sing:

> I think of my blessed Redeemer,
> I think of Him all the day long:
> I sing for I cannot be silent,
> His love is the theme of my song.

19 Shipwreck

Suggested Scripture: Psalm 16

Standing stark above swirling white waters on the Saumarex Reef is the rust-rotted ruin of the U.S. Liberty Ship *Francis Preston Blair*. Some eighty feet separate this forlorn wreckage from the sea since it was blown there by a violent hurricane in 1945. From the distance it still looks like a ship underway rather than the ruin it is. On the ocean side, a few hundred yards away, cobalt breakers as big as houses explode in slow frost-white cataclysm and thunder. Salvage of the great ship is impractical since cost would be prohibitive. And so it stands, losing the battle against time, eventually to be swallowed by the elements.

Shipwreck is a word striking terror in hearts of men of the sea and land alike. Ships are the largest conveyance of people and cargo of any mode of transportation, and they never become castaways without dramatic results. There are few parts of the world's coastal regions without bleached bones of broken vessels.

Even the largest and most pretentious vessels are not impervious to the whims of the waters. Authorities assured people that the *Titanic* would never sink; but it did, taking over fourteen hundred lives with it. The winds and the waves refuse to be mastered. Lord Byron wisely penned:

Roll on, thou deep and dark blue ocean—roll!
  Ten thousand fleets sweep over thee in vain:

59

> Man marks the earth with ruin—his control
>> Stops with the shore.

Wise to the ways of the waves, the apostle Paul draws on this knowledge to warn young Timothy of the destructive breakers of sin: "Holding faith, and a good conscience; which some having put away concerning faith have made shipwreck" (I Tim. 1:19). In other words, just as the liberty ship was blown helplessly on the high coral, so our lives can be wrecked and ruined by winds and waves of passion. A walk down any city street gives tragic testimony to this truth. Very apparent are ruined lives rotting and rusting on the corals of sin, losing their personal battle against time. These are the walking dead, hopelessly locked in their loneliness on their own particular coral reef of despair. Too many of them die left all alone, their lives washed up forever on the sharp rocks of defeat.

Many feel they can successfully master winds and waves. They feel that the driving forces of their own lives—intellectualism, security, position, or prominence—will keep them from the shoals. However, none of these is guarantee that their lives will not end up on the corals of death. William Ernest Henley proudly penned:

> Beyond this place of wrath and tears
>> Looms but the horror of the shade,
> And yet the menace of the years
>> Finds, and shall find me unafraid.

Yet he died a suicide, learning too late he was not the master of his fate or the captain of his soul.

Lest we despair, there is a force greater than winds and waves of sin. Christ one day was sleeping in the bow of a boat when the seas began to churn. Frightened, the disciples awakened Him, crying, "Carest thou not that we perish?" In that moment He proved He was Lord of all by simply stating, "Peace, be still." The Bible says, "And the wind ceased, and there was a great calm" (see Mark 4:37-39).

Although our lives are driven by mighty forces that would shipwreck us, there is a Master of the ship who can always be with us to calm the seas. He can also salvage those who have been stranded on shoals of despair, making them seaworthy again. God said that His Son would "give unto them beauty for ashes, the oil of joy for mourning, the garment of praise for the spirit of heaviness" (Isa. 61:3). No wonder the songwriter could sing:

> Whether the wrath of the storm-tossed sea,
>   Or demons or men, or whatever it be,
> No water can swallow the ship where lies
>   The Master of ocean, and earth, and skies;
> They all shall sweetly obey His will,
>   Peace be still, Peace be still.

20 First Day in Heaven

Suggested Scripture: Philippians 2:1-16

The other day I ran across the following little poem by an unknown author that preaches a sermon so clearly none can misunderstand.

> I dreamed death came the other night;
>   And heaven's gates swung wide.
> With kindly grace an angel
>   Ushered me inside.
> And there, to my astonishment,
>   Stood folks I'd known on earth.
> Some I'd judged and labeled
>   Unfit or of little worth.
> Indignant words rose to my lips,
>   But never were set free;
> For every face showed stunned surprise . . .
>   No one expected me!

All of us seem to have an uncanny ability to detect flaws or weaknesses in others' behavior, yet seldom see our own. It is a problem as old as sin and yet as new as this morning's sunrise. The Bible speaks much about this tendency to judge without justice.

Paul pondered to the Ephesians: "Be humble and gentle. Be patient with each other, making allowance for each other's faults because of your love" (4:2, The Living Bible). Jesus further pressed home the point by stating, "Don't criticize, and then you won't be criticized. For others will treat you as you treat them. And why worry about a speck in the eye of a brother when you have a board in your own? Should you say, 'Friend, let me help you get that speck out of your own eye?' when you can't even see because of the board in your own? Hypocrite! First get rid of the board. Then you can see to help your brother" (Matt. 7:1-4, The Living Bible).

Yet the problem is more complex than it seems. Doesn't the Bible also say, "He that justifieth the wicked, and he that condemneth the just, even they both are abomination to the Lord" (Prov. 17:15)? Therefore, are we to overlook evil and actually let it prevail because we are not to judge? Obviously, Christ did not intend for there to be a passive attitude toward evil. He lashed out against those polluting the temple, demanding repentance. What Christ clearly demands is that we clean up our own lives before we are qualified to ride against the evil of our times.

Today we are overcrowded with crusades against various evils. Hundreds of groups have sprung up to fight the drug culture. Yet those involved with drugs rightly ask, "How can a generation hooked on alcohol condemn our use of drugs?" And of course there is no reasonable answer. The problem becomes plainer when the man who robs a grocer with a gun is trying to be rehabilitated by one who robs the government by cheating on his taxes. This level of hypocrisy is in all of our society and may be the root reason why youth are rebelling and questioning our right to tell them what they should not do. It is easy to understand their anger.

However, evil does exist and the drug problem is reaching epidemic proportions in some areas. Crimes rage in the streets and we are becoming a lawless society. Obviously, something must be done against evil for our survival. Lest we despair, there is an answer. Christ taught that sin was to be stopped on a personal level, with individuals living lives of righteousness. Merely articulating the wrong of others does not heal. After all, society is merely made up of *us* and will never rise any higher than one's own righteousness. If real cure comes it must be a rising flood of personal righteousness spilling over against evil. Anything short of this is merely rhetoric.

There is no shortcut to peace. It must come, as God outlines in His Word, first with personal righteousness. We then move from self-righteous snobs passing value judgments on others to responsible individuals who are really effective against evil.